The scenery of mountains painted on the ever-changing azure canvas of the sky, the mysterious mechanism of the human body, the rose, the green grass carpet, the magnanimity of souls, the loftiness of minds, the depth of love—all these things remind us of a God who is beautiful and noble.

—Paramahansa Yogananda

THE PHOTOGRAPHS IN THIS CALENDAR are accompanied by selections from the writings of Paramahansa Yogananda, whose timeless and universal teachings have awakened many, of all races, cultures, and creeds, to a deeper awareness of the one reality that sustains and unites us all.

Whether spread over the vast heavens or hidden in the exquisite delicacy of a tiny flower, nature's beauty is always beckoning, inviting us to look behind the outward form and sense the presence of God within.

We hope that the thoughts and images in these pages will bring you inspiration and encouragement in the days and weeks of the coming year.

Whahariki Beach, Golden Bay, New Zealand   Photograph by Steffen & Alexandra Sailer/AnimalsAnimals

*B*ehold, through the gates of the New Year, the distant variegated decorations of future achievements glimmering at you and daringly luring you to give pursuit.

—Paramahansa Yogananda

Fresh snow, Nordland County, Norway   Photograph by Kevin McNeal

December/January

28
monday

Boxing Day (U.K., Australia, N.Z. – Observed)

Things I'm looking for in a mate:

1) College educated

2) loves God, is spiritual in a big way

29
tuesday

3) Loves & cares for his family

4) Stable in job, finances & income

30
wednesday

5) generous, giving personality

6) Kind to people

7) Honest & trustworthy

31
thursday

8) Real, He keeps it 100 good or bad

9) Good communicator I can talk to him about everything

1
friday

New Year's Day   Last Quarter ◑

10) Emotionally available

DECEMBER 2015

S	M	T	W	T	F	S
		1	2	3	4	5
6	7	8	9	10	11	12
13	14	15	16	17	18	19
20	21	22	23	24	25	26
27	28	29	30	31		

JANUARY

S	M	T	W	T	F	S
					1	2
3	4	5	6	7	8	9
10	11	12	13	14	15	16
17	18	19	20	21	22	23
24/31	25	26	27	28	29	30

Looks

1) Good teeth

2) Well groomed

2
saturday

3) Tall

4) Hair

5) Nice eyes

3
sunday

January

4
monday
Set goals - the goal will draw you to it like a magnet.
Day After New Year's Day (N.Z. – Observed)

5
tuesday
Blocked chakras
Solar Plexus downwards
Paramahansa Yogananda's Birthday

6
wednesday
Routine
warm water
oil pulling
yoga
meditation every morning

7
thursday

8
friday

9
saturday
New Moon ●

10
sunday

JANUARY

S	M	T	W	T	F	S
					1	2
3	4	5	6	7	8	9
10	11	12	13	14	15	16
17	18	19	20	21	22	23
24/31	25	26	27	28	29	30

FEBRUARY

S	M	T	W	T	F	S
	1	2	3	4	5	6
7	8	9	10	11	12	13
14	15	16	17	18	19	20
21	22	23	24	25	26	27
28	29					

The purpose of meditation is to calm the mind,
that without distortion it may mirror Omnipresence.

—Paramahansa Yogananda

Black-necked Stilt and pelicans, Salton Sea, California   Photograph by John Hendrickson

In the airplane of your visualization, glide over the limitless empire of thoughts. There behold the mountain ranges of unbroken, lofty, spiritual aspirations.

—Paramahansa Yogananda

Sunrise, Upper Tipsoo Lake, Mt. Rainier National Park, Washington   Photograph by Kevin McNeal

January

11
monday

jobs

flight attendant
make up
interior design

12
tuesday

inner

energy healing
Ayurveda
Taste therapy

13
wednesday

Harithaki
Bitter gourd.

14
thursday

mind

intentions
goals
I ams

15
friday

pulling power back
Anger / substances / mental
↓ watch these

First Quarter ◐

16
saturday

17
sunday

JANUARY

S	M	T	W	T	F	S
					1	2
3	4	5	6	7	8	9
10	11	12	13	14	15	16
17	18	19	20	21	22	23
24/31	25	26	27	28	29	30

FEBRUARY

S	M	T	W	T	F	S
	1	2	3	4	5	6
7	8	9	10	11	12	13
14	15	16	17	18	19	20
21	22	23	24	25	26	27
28	29					

January

18
monday

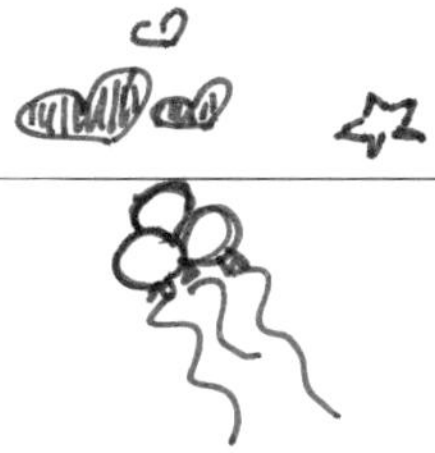

Martin Luther King, Jr.'s Birthday (Observed)

19
tuesday

oil pulling

Harithaki cleanse
Homeopathic gall bladder detox w/ epsom salts

20
wednesday

coffee enema

21
thursday

This week

Tysons
Nails.
Threading
Facial.

22
friday

23
saturday

Full Moon ○

24
sunday

JANUARY

S	M	T	W	T	F	S
					1	2
3	4	5	6	7	8	9
10	11	12	13	14	15	16
17	18	19	20	21	22	23
24/31	25	26	27	28	29	30

FEBRUARY

S	M	T	W	T	F	S
	1	2	3	4	5	6
7	8	9	10	11	12	13
14	15	16	17	18	19	20
21	22	23	24	25	26	27
28	29					

Remain calm, serene, always in command of yourself. You will then find out how easy it is to get along.

—Paramahansa Yogananda

Female Northern Cardinal and hawthorn berries, Louisville, Kentucky
Photograph by Adam Jones/Dennis Flaherty Photography

Inspiration, creative power, and energy flow into you
when you attune yourself to the Infinite Mind during meditation.

—Paramahansa Yogananda

Sunrise, Godafoss Waterfall, Iceland Photograph by Dennis Kirkland/Jaynes Gallery

January

25 monday

Focus on doing you until someone comes along and helps you do you even better.

26 tuesday

Australia Day (Australia)

27 wednesday

Nightly Detox tea

1/2 cup ginger
1/2 cup turmeric fresh
5 cloves

→ cheese cloth tied w/ kitchen string

28 thursday

1 chammomile tea

Add to 2 cups water boiling

29 friday

Steep 20 min
Remove spices
1/2 lemon
1 tsp coconut oil
raw honey

→ add to tea

30 saturday

31 sunday

Last Quarter ◑

January						
S	M	T	W	T	F	S
					1	2
3	4	5	6	7	8	9
10	11	12	13	14	15	16
17	18	19	20	21	22	23
24/31	25	26	27	28	29	30

February						
S	M	T	W	T	F	S
	1	2	3	4	5	6
7	8	9	10	11	12	13
14	15	16	17	18	19	20
21	22	23	24	25	26	27
28	29					

February

1
monday

2
tuesday

3
wednesday

4
thursday

5
friday

6
saturday

7
sunday

FEBRUARY

S	M	T	W	T	F	S
	1	2	3	4	5	6
7	8	9	10	11	12	13
14	15	16	17	18	19	20
21	22	23	24	25	26	27
28	29					

MARCH

S	M	T	W	T	F	S
		1	2	3	4	5
6	7	8	9	10	11	12
13	14	15	16	17	18	19
20	21	22	23	24	25	26
27	28	29	30	31		

Underlying all life is the silent voice of God, ever calling to us through flowers, through scriptures, and through our conscience — through all things that are beautiful and that make life worth living.

—Paramahansa Yogananda

Water lily, Erie, Pennsylvania   Photograph by Ellen Anon

Ignite our earthliness with the flame of infinity....
Inflame our minds with Thy thoughts! Inflame our hearts with Thy love!
Inflame our souls with Thy joy!

—Paramahansa Yogananda

Lava burst, Pu'u O'o vent, Kilauea volcano, Hawaii   Photograph by G. Brad Lewis

February

Waitangi Day (N.Z. – Observed) New Moon ●

8
monday

9
tuesday

10
wednesday

11
thursday

Lincoln's Birthday

12
friday

February

S	M	T	W	T	F	S
	1	2	3	4	5	6
7	8	9	10	11	12	13
14	15	16	17	18	19	20
21	22	23	24	25	26	27
28	29					

13
saturday

March

S	M	T	W	T	F	S
		1	2	3	4	5
6	7	8	9	10	11	12
13	14	15	16	17	18	19
20	21	22	23	24	25	26
27	28	29	30	31		

St. Valentine's Day First Quarter ◐

14
sunday

February

15
monday

Presidents' Day

16
tuesday

17
wednesday

18
thursday

19
friday

20
saturday

21
sunday

FEBRUARY

S	M	T	W	T	F	S
	1	2	3	4	5	6
7	8	9	10	11	12	13
14	15	16	17	18	19	20
21	22	23	24	25	26	27
28	29					

MARCH

S	M	T	W	T	F	S
		1	2	3	4	5
6	7	8	9	10	11	12
13	14	15	16	17	18	19
20	21	22	23	24	25	26
27	28	29	30	31		

When the mind becomes still, you are in the kingdom of the Infinite.

—Paramahansa Yogananda

El Capitan, Yosemite National Park, California   Photograph by Mary Liz Austin

You are, and ever shall be, a perfect reflection of Spirit.

—Paramahansa Yogananda

Chobe National Park, Botswana, Africa Photograph by Franz Lanting/Photoshot

February

22
monday

Washington's Birthday Full Moon ○

23
tuesday

24
wednesday

25
thursday

26
friday

FEBRUARY

S	M	T	W	T	F	S
	1	2	3	4	5	6
7	8	9	10	11	12	13
14	15	16	17	18	19	20
21	22	23	24	25	26	27
28	29					

MARCH

S	M	T	W	T	F	S
		1	2	3	4	5
6	7	8	9	10	11	12
13	14	15	16	17	18	19
20	21	22	23	24	25	26
27	28	29	30	31		

27
saturday

28
sunday

February/March

29
monday

1
tuesday
Last Quarter ◑

2
wednesday

3
thursday

4
friday

5
saturday

6
sunday
Mothering Sunday (U.K.)

February

S	M	T	W	T	F	S
	1	2	3	4	5	6
7	8	9	10	11	12	13
14	15	16	17	18	19	20
21	22	23	24	25	26	27
28	29					

March

S	M	T	W	T	F	S
		1	2	3	4	5
6	7	8	9	10	11	12
13	14	15	16	17	18	19
20	21	22	23	24	25	26
27	28	29	30	31		

When you know that beneath the wave of your life is the great Ocean of Life, and beneath your joy the bliss of God—then you are really living.

—Paramahansa Yogananda

Cape Kiwanda, Oregon   Photograph by Dennis Frates

Find friendship with your true Self, the soul, in the sanctum of daily meditation;
and after deep communion with God in the bower of peace,
give divine friendship and goodwill to all.

—Paramahansa Yogananda

Moss-covered trees, Lacassine National Wildlife Refuge, Louisiana   Photograph by Michael Jones/AKM Images

March

7
monday
Paramahansa Yogananda's Mahasamadhi

8
tuesday
New Moon ●

9
wednesday
Sri Yukteswar's Mahasamadhi

10
thursday

11
friday

12
saturday

13
sunday
Daylight Saving Time begins (U.S. and Canada)

MARCH

S	M	T	W	T	F	S
		1	2	3	4	5
6	7	8	9	10	11	12
13	14	15	16	17	18	19
20	21	22	23	24	25	26
27	28	29	30	31		

APRIL

S	M	T	W	T	F	S
					1	2
3	4	5	6	7	8	9
10	11	12	13	14	15	16
17	18	19	20	21	22	23
24	25	26	27	28	29	30

March

14
monday

15
tuesday
First Quarter ◐

16
wednesday

17
thursday
St. Patrick's Day

18
friday

19
saturday
Vernal Equinox

20
sunday

March

S	M	T	W	T	F	S
		1	2	3	4	5
6	7	8	9	10	11	12
13	14	15	16	17	18	19
20	21	22	23	24	25	26
27	28	29	30	31		

April

S	M	T	W	T	F	S
					1	2
3	4	5	6	7	8	9
10	11	12	13	14	15	16
17	18	19	20	21	22	23
24	25	26	27	28	29	30

Have you ever analyzed your mental diet?
It consists usually of the thoughts which you are thinking
as well as the thoughts that you are receiving
from the close thought contact with your friends.

—Paramahansa Yogananda

Male Scrub Euphonia, Honduras   Photograph by Fi Rust

Every motivation is good that brings forth a flower of God's manifest qualities and understanding....If someone is suffering and you reach out with aid and compassion, you are moving into the presence of God.

—Paramahansa Yogananda

Ornamental oregano, Seabeck, Washington   Photograph by Don Paulson

March

21
monday

22
tuesday

Full Moon ○

23
wednesday

24
thursday

Good Friday

25
friday

MARCH

S	M	T	W	T	F	S
		1	2	3	4	5
6	7	8	9	10	11	12
13	14	15	16	17	18	19
20	21	22	23	24	25	26
27	28	29	30	31		

26
saturday

APRIL

S	M	T	W	T	F	S
					1	2
3	4	5	6	7	8	9
10	11	12	13	14	15	16
17	18	19	20	21	22	23
24	25	26	27	28	29	30

Easter Sunday Daylight Saving Time begins (European Union)

27
sunday

March/April

28
monday

Easter Monday (Canada, U.K., Australia, N.Z.)

29
tuesday

30
wednesday

31
thursday

Last Quarter ◑

1
friday

2
saturday

3
sunday

March

S	M	T	W	T	F	S
		1	2	3	4	5
6	7	8	9	10	11	12
13	14	15	16	17	18	19
20	21	22	23	24	25	26
27	28	29	30	31		

April

S	M	T	W	T	F	S
					1	2
3	4	5	6	7	8	9
10	11	12	13	14	15	16
17	18	19	20	21	22	23
24	25	26	27	28	29	30

When by meditation techniques we withdraw restless thoughts from the lake of the mind, we behold our soul, a perfect reflection of Spirit, and realize that the soul and God are One.

—Paramahansa Yogananda

Lago del Predil, Julian Alps, Italy   Photograph by Guy Edwardes

By right living, right thinking, and meditation you can race to the Infinite.

—Paramahansa Yogananda

Red lechwe, Okavango Delta, Botswana   Photograph by Franz Lanting

April

4
monday

5
tuesday

6
wednesday

New Moon ●

7
thursday

8
friday

APRIL

S	M	T	W	T	F	S
					1	2
3	4	5	6	7	8	9
10	11	12	13	14	15	16
17	18	19	20	21	22	23
24	25	26	27	28	29	30

MAY

S	M	T	W	T	F	S
1	2	3	4	5	6	7
8	9	10	11	12	13	14
15	16	17	18	19	20	21
22	23	24	25	26	27	28
29	30	31				

9
saturday

10
sunday

April

11
monday

12
tuesday

13
wednesday
First Quarter ◐

14
thursday

15
friday

16
saturday

17
sunday

APRIL

S	M	T	W	T	F	S
					1	2
3	4	5	6	7	8	9
10	11	12	13	14	15	16
17	18	19	20	21	22	23
24	25	26	27	28	29	30

MAY

S	M	T	W	T	F	S
1	2	3	4	5	6	7
8	9	10	11	12	13	14
15	16	17	18	19	20	21
22	23	24	25	26	27	28
29	30	31				

In each soul is the unique imprint of the grace of God.
Nowhere in the world is there another exactly like you.

—Paramahansa Yogananda

White Admiral butterly, Adirondacks, New York   Photograph by Robert Lubeck/AnimalsAnimals

Whatever you want to be, start to develop that pattern now.
You can instill any trend in your consciousness right now,
provided you inject a strong thought in your mind;
then your actions and whole being will obey that thought.

—Paramahansa Yogananda

Padre Bay, Lake Powell, Utah Photograph by Don Paulson

April

18
monday

19
tuesday

20
wednesday

Full Moon ○
21
thursday

Earth Day Passover begins
22
friday

APRIL

S	M	T	W	T	F	S
					1	2
3	4	5	6	7	8	9
10	11	12	13	14	15	16
17	18	19	20	21	22	23
24	25	26	27	28	29	30

23
saturday

MAY

S	M	T	W	T	F	S
1	2	3	4	5	6	7
8	9	10	11	12	13	14
15	16	17	18	19	20	21
22	23	24	25	26	27	28
29	30	31				

24
sunday

April/May

25
monday

ANZAC Day (Australia and N.Z.)

26
tuesday

27
wednesday

28
thursday

29
friday

Last Quarter ◑

30
saturday

1
sunday

April

S	M	T	W	T	F	S
					1	2
3	4	5	6	7	8	9
10	11	12	13	14	15	16
17	18	19	20	21	22	23
24	25	26	27	28	29	30

May

S	M	T	W	T	F	S
1	2	3	4	5	6	7
8	9	10	11	12	13	14
15	16	17	18	19	20	21
22	23	24	25	26	27	28
29	30	31				

True calmness means that God is with you....
If you remain inwardly calm,
you are demonstrating the poise of a true child of God.

—Paramahansa Yogananda

Great Blue Heron, Victoria, British Columbia   Photograph by Michael Wheatley

The mother's love is not given to us to spoil us with indulgence, but to soften our hearts, that we may in turn soften others with kindness.

—Paramahansa Yogananda

Mother grizzly bear with cubs, Lake Clark National Park, Alaska   Photograph by Daisy Gilardini/Getty Images

May

Early May Bank Holiday (U.K.) — 2 monday

3 tuesday

4 wednesday

National Day of Prayer — 5 thursday

New Moon ● — 6 friday

7 saturday

Mother's Day (U.S., Canada, Australia, N.Z.) — 8 sunday

May

S	M	T	W	T	F	S
1	2	3	4	5	6	7
8	9	10	11	12	13	14
15	16	17	18	19	20	21
22	23	24	25	26	27	28
29	30	31				

June

S	M	T	W	T	F	S
			1	2	3	4
5	6	7	8	9	10	11
12	13	14	15	16	17	18
19	20	21	22	23	24	25
26	27	28	29	30		

9
monday

10
tuesday
Sri Yukteswar's Birthday

11
wednesday

12
thursday

13
friday
First Quarter ◐

14
saturday

15
sunday

MAY

S	M	T	W	T	F	S
1	2	3	4	5	6	7
8	9	10	11	12	13	14
15	16	17	18	19	20	21
22	23	24	25	26	27	28
29	30	31				

JUNE

S	M	T	W	T	F	S
			1	2	3	4
5	6	7	8	9	10	11
12	13	14	15	16	17	18
19	20	21	22	23	24	25
26	27	28	29	30		

It is time we retrace our footsteps Home and reach finally that divine Kingdom wherein we shall be free from all suffering and heartaches.

—Paramahansa Yogananda

Eastern Sierra Nevada mountains, California Photograph by Dennis Flaherty

When one contemplates the expanse of ocean and sky, he escapes momentarily the confinements of finite matter and glimpses the Infinite.

—Paramahansa Yogananda

Whahariki Beach, Golden Bay, New Zealand   Photograph by Minden Pictures/SuperStock

May

16
monday

17
tuesday

18
wednesday

19
thursday

20
friday

MAY

S	M	T	W	T	F	S
1	2	3	4	5	6	7
8	9	10	11	12	13	14
15	16	17	18	19	20	21
22	23	24	25	26	27	28
29	30	31				

JUNE

S	M	T	W	T	F	S
			1	2	3	4
5	6	7	8	9	10	11
12	13	14	15	16	17	18
19	20	21	22	23	24	25
26	27	28	29	30		

21
saturday

Full Moon ○

22
sunday

23
monday
Victoria Day (Canada)

24
tuesday

25
wednesday

26
thursday

27
friday

28
saturday

29
sunday
Last Quarter ◑

May

S	M	T	W	T	F	S
1	2	3	4	5	6	7
8	9	10	11	12	13	14
15	16	17	18	19	20	21
22	23	24	25	26	27	28
29	30	31				

June

S	M	T	W	T	F	S
			1	2	3	4
5	6	7	8	9	10	11
12	13	14	15	16	17	18
19	20	21	22	23	24	25
26	27	28	29	30		

God the Beautiful is manifest in the synchronized scenery of nature.
His breath is heaving in the wind;
His divinity is smiling at us in the flowers.
The qualities of love and peace and joy that grow in the garden of human hearts
are reflecting His goodness, His beauty.

—Paramahansa Yogananda

Lupine meadows, Mt. Rainier National Park, Washington Photograph by Kevin McNeal

Like a silent invisible river flowing beneath the desert, flows the vast dimensionless river of Spirit, through the sands of time, through the sands of experience, through the sands of all souls, through the sands of all living atoms, through the sands of all space.

—Paramahansa Yogananda

Namib-Naukluft National Park, Namibia Photograph by Franz Lanting

May/June

30
monday

Memorial Day Spring Bank Holiday (U.K.)

31
tuesday

1
wednesday

2
thursday

3
friday

4
saturday

New Moon ●

5
sunday

May

S	M	T	W	T	F	S
1	2	3	4	5	6	7
8	9	10	11	12	13	14
15	16	17	18	19	20	21
22	23	24	25	26	27	28
29	30	31				

June

S	M	T	W	T	F	S
			1	2	3	4
5	6	7	8	9	10	11
12	13	14	15	16	17	18
19	20	21	22	23	24	25
26	27	28	29	30		

6
monday
Queen's Birthday (N.Z.)

7
tuesday

8
wednesday

9
thursday

10
friday

11
saturday

12
sunday
First Quarter ◐

JUNE

S	M	T	W	T	F	S
			1	2	3	4
5	6	7	8	9	10	11
12	13	14	15	16	17	18
19	20	21	22	23	24	25
26	27	28	29	30		

JULY

S	M	T	W	T	F	S
					1	2
3	4	5	6	7	8	9
10	11	12	13	14	15	16
17	18	19	20	21	22	23
24/31	25	26	27	28	29	30

Live each present moment completely and the future will take care of itself.
Fully enjoy the wonder and beauty of each instant.
Practice the presence of peace. The more you do that,
the more you will feel the presence of that power in your life.

—Paramahansa Yogananda

Black-chinned hummingbird, Arizona   Photograph by Jackie Klieger

You may be surprised at what seclusion with God
will do for your mind, body and soul.
In the early morning, and before retiring,
you should immerse yourself in His peace.

—Paramahansa Yogananda

Tiger, Corbett National Park, India   Photograph by Martin Harvey/DRK Photo

June

Queen's Birthday (Australia)

13
monday

14
tuesday

15
wednesday

16
thursday

17
friday

June

S	M	T	W	T	F	S
			1	2	3	4
5	6	7	8	9	10	11
12	13	14	15	16	17	18
19	20	21	22	23	24	25
26	27	28	29	30		

July

S	M	T	W	T	F	S
					1	2
3	4	5	6	7	8	9
10	11	12	13	14	15	16
17	18	19	20	21	22	23
24/31	25	26	27	28	29	30

18
saturday

Father's Day (U.S., Canada, U.K.)

19
sunday

June

20
monday
Summer Solstice   Full Moon ○

21
tuesday
International Day of Yoga

22
wednesday

23
thursday

24
friday

25
saturday

26
sunday

June

S	M	T	W	T	F	S
			1	2	3	4
5	6	7	8	9	10	11
12	13	14	15	16	17	18
19	20	21	22	23	24	25
26	27	28	29	30		

July

S	M	T	W	T	F	S
					1	2
3	4	5	6	7	8	9
10	11	12	13	14	15	16
17	18	19	20	21	22	23
24/31	25	26	27	28	29	30

Let us leave the confines of ego and wander in the vast fields of soul progress.
As time is marching on, so must your souls march on
to a greater expansion of your life in Spirit.

—Paramahansa Yogananda

Lavender field, Sault, France Photograph by Guy Edwardes

Day by day, as you learn to meditate, a new awakening will come;
a new, living relationship with God will be established.
The mist of silence and mystery which hangs over everything
will slowly vanish before the dawning light
of your mental and devotional search for God.

—Paramahansa Yogananda

Morning mist, Sudbury, Ontario, Canada   Photograph by Carl Hanninen/Grandmaison Photography

June/July

Last Quarter ◑

27
monday

28
tuesday

29
wednesday

30
thursday

Canada Day (Canada)

1
friday

2
saturday

3
sunday

JUNE

S	M	T	W	T	F	S
			1	2	3	4
5	6	7	8	9	10	11
12	13	14	15	16	17	18
19	20	21	22	23	24	25
26	27	28	29	30		

JULY

S	M	T	W	T	F	S
					1	2
3	4	5	6	7	8	9
10	11	12	13	14	15	16
17	18	19	20	21	22	23
24/31	25	26	27	28	29	30

July

4
monday

New Moon ● Independence Day

5
tuesday

6
wednesday

7
thursday

8
friday

9
saturday

10
sunday

JULY

S	M	T	W	T	F	S
					1	2
3	4	5	6	7	8	9
10	11	12	13	14	15	16
17	18	19	20	21	22	23
24/31	25	26	27	28	29	30

AUGUST

S	M	T	W	T	F	S
	1	2	3	4	5	6
7	8	9	10	11	12	13
14	15	16	17	18	19	20
21	22	23	24	25	26	27
28	29	30	31			

Think that which is good; love that which is good.
Be enthroned in the castle of goodness,
and your memories will be like beautiful flowers
in a garden of noble dreams.

—Paramahansa Yogananda

Flowering redbud, Merced River Canyon, California   Photograph by Terry Donnelly

One who gives mental and material help to others
with a heart overflowing with kindness
will find the same coming back to him.

—Paramahansa Yogananda

Seljalandsfoss waterfall, Iceland Photograph by Guy Edwardes

July

First Quarter ◐

11
monday

12
tuesday

13
wednesday

14
thursday

15
friday

July

S	M	T	W	T	F	S
					1	2
3	4	5	6	7	8	9
10	11	12	13	14	15	16
17	18	19	20	21	22	23
24/31	25	26	27	28	29	30

August

S	M	T	W	T	F	S
	1	2	3	4	5	6
7	8	9	10	11	12	13
14	15	16	17	18	19	20
21	22	23	24	25	26	27
28	29	30	31			

16
saturday

17
sunday

July

18
monday

19
tuesday
Full Moon ○

20
wednesday

21
thursday

22
friday

23
saturday

24
sunday

JULY

S	M	T	W	T	F	S
					1	2
3	4	5	6	7	8	9
10	11	12	13	14	15	16
17	18	19	20	21	22	23
24/31	25	26	27	28	29	30

AUGUST

S	M	T	W	T	F	S
	1	2	3	4	5	6
7	8	9	10	11	12	13
14	15	16	17	18	19	20
21	22	23	24	25	26	27
28	29	30	31			

When the Spirit is known, and when we know ourselves as Spirit,
there is no land or sea, no earth or sky — all is He.

—Paramahansa Yogananda

Salton Sea National Wildlife Refuge, California   Photograph by Cliff Beittel

It is the naughty baby who cries the loudest
that gets his mother's attention first.
So be like the naughty baby and cry for God.
Be satisfied with nothing less than God.

—Paramahansa Yogananda

Lioness and cubs, Maasai Mara National Reserve, Kenya   Photograph by Anup Shah

July

25
monday

Mahavatar Babaji Commemoration Day

26
tuesday

Last Quarter ◑

27
wednesday

28
thursday

29
friday

JULY

S	M	T	W	T	F	S
					1	2
3	4	5	6	7	8	9
10	11	12	13	14	15	16
17	18	19	20	21	22	23
24/31	25	26	27	28	29	30

AUGUST

S	M	T	W	T	F	S
	1	2	3	4	5	6
7	8	9	10	11	12	13
14	15	16	17	18	19	20
21	22	23	24	25	26	27
28	29	30	31			

30
saturday

31
sunday

August

1
monday

Summer Bank Holiday (Scotland)

2
tuesday

New Moon ●

3
wednesday

4
thursday

5
friday

6
saturday

7
sunday

AUGUST

S	M	T	W	T	F	S
	1	2	3	4	5	6
7	8	9	10	11	12	13
14	15	16	17	18	19	20
21	22	23	24	25	26	27
28	29	30	31			

SEPTEMBER

S	M	T	W	T	F	S
				1	2	3
4	5	6	7	8	9	10
11	12	13	14	15	16	17
18	19	20	21	22	23	24
25	26	27	28	29	30	

Heaven on earth is found only within by the contact
of the illuminating Immutable Wisdom perceived in meditation....
Find the heavenly land of infinity within.

—Paramahansa Yogananda

Rainbow over Tunnels Beach, Kauai   Photograph by Jon Cornforth

Remember only the beautiful things that you have felt,
and seen, and experienced.
If your five senses behold only the good,
then your mind will be a garden of blossoming soul qualities.

—Paramahansa Yogananda

Water lilies, Hughes Water Gardens, Oregon   Photograph by Dennis Frates

August

8
monday

9
tuesday

First Quarter ◐

10
wednesday

11
thursday

12
friday

August

S	M	T	W	T	F	S
	1	2	3	4	5	6
7	8	9	10	11	12	13
14	15	16	17	18	19	20
21	22	23	24	25	26	27
28	29	30	31			

13
saturday

September

S	M	T	W	T	F	S
				1	2	3
4	5	6	7	8	9	10
11	12	13	14	15	16	17
18	19	20	21	22	23	24
25	26	27	28	29	30	

14
sunday

August

15
monday

16
tuesday

17
wednesday

18
thursday

Full Moon ◯

19
friday

20
saturday

21
sunday

AUGUST

S	M	T	W	T	F	S
	1	2	3	4	5	6
7	8	9	10	11	12	13
14	15	16	17	18	19	20
21	22	23	24	25	26	27
28	29	30	31			

SEPTEMBER

S	M	T	W	T	F	S
				1	2	3
4	5	6	7	8	9	10
11	12	13	14	15	16	17
18	19	20	21	22	23	24
25	26	27	28	29	30	

Remember in meditation that you are one with the vast Spirit....
In that omniscient light of divine recollection,
you shall not only remember—
you shall realize that you are the Infinite Spirit.

—Paramahansa Yogananda

Lion at dusk, Serengeti National Park, Tanzania   Photograph by Anup Shah

God is ever new Joy. This Joy is omnipresent....
Beyond the gross vibratory boundaries of matter,
the Immutable Infinite reigns in all His majesty and vastness.

—Paramahansa Yogananda

Passing storm, Sawtooth Mountains National Recreation Area, Idaho Photograph by Dennis Frates

August

22
monday

23
tuesday

Last Quarter ◑

24
wednesday

Janmashtami

25
thursday

26
friday

AUGUST

S	M	T	W	T	F	S
	1	2	3	4	5	6
7	8	9	10	11	12	13
14	15	16	17	18	19	20
21	22	23	24	25	26	27
28	29	30	31			

SEPTEMBER

S	M	T	W	T	F	S
				1	2	3
4	5	6	7	8	9	10
11	12	13	14	15	16	17
18	19	20	21	22	23	24
25	26	27	28	29	30	

27
saturday

28
sunday

August/September

29
monday
Summer Bank Holiday (England, Wales & N. Ireland)

30
tuesday

31
wednesday

1
thursday
New Moon ●

2
friday

3
saturday

4
sunday
Father's Day (Australia and N.Z.)

AUGUST

S	M	T	W	T	F	S
	1	2	3	4	5	6
7	8	9	10	11	12	13
14	15	16	17	18	19	20
21	22	23	24	25	26	27
28	29	30	31			

SEPTEMBER

S	M	T	W	T	F	S
				1	2	3
4	5	6	7	8	9	10
11	12	13	14	15	16	17
18	19	20	21	22	23	24
25	26	27	28	29	30	

When you have found your true soul-nature of everlasting joy,
that indestructible bliss will remain with you throughout all experiences of life.

—Paramahansa Yogananda

California Sister butterfly, Sierra Nevada foothills, California Photograph by John Hendrickson

The greatest thing in life is to live in the castle of your own clear conscience.

—Paramahansa Yogananda

Cathedral Rock, Sedona, Arizona   Photograph by Prisma/Superstock

September

5
monday

Labor Day (U.S. and Canada)

6
tuesday

7
wednesday

8
thursday

9
friday

First Quarter ◐

10
saturday

11
sunday

September

S	M	T	W	T	F	S
				1	2	3
4	5	6	7	8	9	10
11	12	13	14	15	16	17
18	19	20	21	22	23	24
25	26	27	28	29	30	

October

S	M	T	W	T	F	S
						1
2	3	4	5	6	7	8
9	10	11	12	13	14	15
16	17	18	19	20	21	22
23/30	24/31	25	26	27	28	29

September

12
monday

13
tuesday

14
wednesday

15
thursday

16
friday

Full Moon ○

17
saturday

18
sunday

SEPTEMBER

S	M	T	W	T	F	S
				1	2	3
4	5	6	7	8	9	10
11	12	13	14	15	16	17
18	19	20	21	22	23	24
25	26	27	28	29	30	

OCTOBER

S	M	T	W	T	F	S
						1
2	3	4	5	6	7	8
9	10	11	12	13	14	15
16	17	18	19	20	21	22
23/30	24/31	25	26	27	28	29

Do your part to make lasting friendships by being a true friend.

—Paramahansa Yogananda

White-tailed deer fawns, Pine County, Minnesota   Photograph by Cathy and Gordon Illg

Soar in the plane of silence over the peaks of highest wisdom,
and roam in the land of endless beauty and happiness.
Arise, awaken your spirit.

—Paramahansa Yogananda

Sunrise, Grand Teton National Park, Wyoming   Photograph by Tom Bean/DRK Photo

September

19
monday

20
tuesday

U.N. International Day of Peace

21
wednesday

Autumnal Equinox

22
thursday

Last Quarter ◑

23
friday

September

S	M	T	W	T	F	S
				1	2	3
4	5	6	7	8	9	10
11	12	13	14	15	16	17
18	19	20	21	22	23	24
25	26	27	28	29	30	

October

S	M	T	W	T	F	S
						1
2	3	4	5	6	7	8
9	10	11	12	13	14	15
16	17	18	19	20	21	22
23/30	24/31	25	26	27	28	29

24
saturday

25
sunday

September/October

26
monday
Lahiri Mahasaya's Mahasamadhi

27
tuesday

28
wednesday

29
thursday

30
friday
Lahiri Mahasaya's Birthday New Moon ●

1
saturday

2
sunday
Rosh Hashanah

SEPTEMBER

S	M	T	W	T	F	S
				1	2	3
4	5	6	7	8	9	10
11	12	13	14	15	16	17
18	19	20	21	22	23	24
25	26	27	28	29	30	

OCTOBER

S	M	T	W	T	F	S
						1
2	3	4	5	6	7	8
9	10	11	12	13	14	15
16	17	18	19	20	21	22
23/30	24/31	25	26	27	28	29

Guide all your actions by the inner voice of spiritual consciousness.

—Paramahansa Yogananda

Mallard ducks landing, Wetumpka, Alabama Photograph by William Houghton/AKM Images

Meditation quiets the waves of feeling so that God's reflection
as the joyous soul is clearly mirrored within.

—Paramahansa Yogananda

Early morning on Snake River, Grand Teton National Park, Wyoming   Photograph by Don Paulson

October

Garbage Disposal
↗

C. Maeys 410-923-0510 Badger 5

3
monday

4
tuesday

pick up Bhoomika's suitcase.

5
wednesday

6
thursday

7
friday

OCTOBER

S	M	T	W	T	F	S
						1
2	3	4	5	6	7	8
9	10	11	12	13	14	15
16	17	18	19	20	21	22
23/30	24/31	25	26	27	28	29

NOVEMBER

S	M	T	W	T	F	S
		1	2	3	4	5
6	7	8	9	10	11	12
13	14	15	16	17	18	19
20	21	22	23	24	25	26
27	28	29	30			

First Quarter ◐

8
saturday

9
sunday

October

10
monday Maryland New Direction Columbus Day Thanksgiving Day (Canada)
2700 N Charles St #200

11
tuesday (TWIC) Federal Transport ID Yom Kippur

12
wednesday Maryland workforce exchange (MWE)

13
thursday

14
friday

15
saturday Full Moon ○

16
sunday

October

S	M	T	W	T	F	S
						1
2	3	4	5	6	7	8
9	10	11	12	13	14	15
16	17	18	19	20	21	22
23/30	24/31	25	26	27	28	29

November

S	M	T	W	T	F	S
		1	2	3	4	5
6	7	8	9	10	11	12
13	14	15	16	17	18	19
20	21	22	23	24	25	26
27	28	29	30			

When two or more persons are friends always, no matter what happens, that is an expression of divine love, or divine friendship.

—Paramahansa Yogananda

Baby elephants, Maasai Mara National Reserve, Kenya   Photograph by Anup Shah

The aurora dancing in the heavens, the mountains,
the glowing furnaces of flame in the sun and stars—
all are but expressions of Thy grace and Thine omnipresence.

—Paramahansa Yogananda

Aurora borealis over Jökulsárlón Glacier Lagoon, Iceland Photograph by Seth Resnick/Superstock

October

17
monday

18
tuesday

19
wednesday

20
thursday

21
friday

Last Quarter ◑

22
saturday

23
sunday

OCTOBER

S	M	T	W	T	F	S
						1
2	3	4	5	6	7	8
9	10	11	12	13	14	15
16	17	18	19	20	21	22
23/30	24/31	25	26	27	28	29

NOVEMBER

S	M	T	W	T	F	S
		1	2	3	4	5
6	7	8	9	10	11	12
13	14	15	16	17	18	19
20	21	22	23	24	25	26
27	28	29	30			

October

24
monday
Labour Day (N.Z.)

25
tuesday

26
wednesday

27
thursday

28
friday

29
saturday

30
sunday
Daylight Saving Time ends (European Union) New Moon ●

OCTOBER

S	M	T	W	T	F	S
						1
2	3	4	5	6	7	8
9	10	11	12	13	14	15
16	17	18	19	20	21	22
23/30	24/31	25	26	27	28	29

NOVEMBER

S	M	T	W	T	F	S
		1	2	3	4	5
6	7	8	9	10	11	12
13	14	15	16	17	18	19
20	21	22	23	24	25	26
27	28	29	30			

God's presence is so close; it is just as though somebody
is playing hide-and-seek with you....
Behind the leaves, behind the wind,
behind the warm rays of the sun — He is hiding, but He is there.

—Paramahansa Yogananda

Autumn forest, Berkshire Mountains, Massachusetts   Photograph by James Randklev

Every person is innately wonderful;
he has only to rid himself of the mask of ego consciousness.

—Paramahansa Yogananda

Cedar waxwing, Bison Range National Wildlife Refuge, Montana   Photograph by Ken Archer

October/November

Halloween (U.S., Canada, U.K.)

31
monday

1
tuesday

2
wednesday

3
thursday

4
friday

OCTOBER

S	M	T	W	T	F	S
						1
2	3	4	5	6	7	8
9	10	11	12	13	14	15
16	17	18	19	20	21	22
23/30	24/31	25	26	27	28	29

NOVEMBER

S	M	T	W	T	F	S
		1	2	3	4	5
6	7	8	9	10	11	12
13	14	15	16	17	18	19
20	21	22	23	24	25	26
27	28	29	30			

5
saturday

Daylight Saving Time ends (U.S. and Canada)

6
sunday

November

7
monday

First Quarter ◐

8
tuesday

General Election Day

9
wednesday

10
thursday

11
friday

Veterans Day   Remembrance Day (Canada)

12
saturday

13
sunday

Remembrance Sunday (U.K.)

NOVEMBER

S	M	T	W	T	F	S
		1	2	3	4	5
6	7	8	9	10	11	12
13	14	15	16	17	18	19
20	21	22	23	24	25	26
27	28	29	30			

DECEMBER

S	M	T	W	T	F	S
				1	2	3
4	5	6	7	8	9	10
11	12	13	14	15	16	17
18	19	20	21	22	23	24
25	26	27	28	29	30	31

In the expression of soul qualities lies the only way to live peacefully....
The power is within us to make home a paradise.

—Paramahansa Yogananda

Bison crossing, Mormon Row, Grand Teton National Park, Wyoming Photograph by Kevin McNeal

Swim in the ocean of vastness and peace and limitless happiness beyond dreams — within yourself.

—Paramahansa Yogananda

Green sea turtle, Balicasag Island, Philippines   Photograph by Tim Fitzharris

November

Full Moon ○

14
monday

15
tuesday

16
wednesday

17
thursday

18
friday

NOVEMBER

S	M	T	W	T	F	S
		1	2	3	4	5
6	7	8	9	10	11	12
13	14	15	16	17	18	19
20	21	22	23	24	25	26
27	28	29	30			

DECEMBER

S	M	T	W	T	F	S
				1	2	3
4	5	6	7	8	9	10
11	12	13	14	15	16	17
18	19	20	21	22	23	24
25	26	27	28	29	30	31

19
saturday

20
sunday

November

21
monday
Last Quarter ◑

22
tuesday

23
wednesday

24
thursday
Thanksgiving Day

25
friday

26
saturday

27
sunday

NOVEMBER

S	M	T	W	T	F	S
		1	2	3	4	5
6	7	8	9	10	11	12
13	14	15	16	17	18	19
20	21	22	23	24	25	26
27	28	29	30			

DECEMBER

S	M	T	W	T	F	S
				1	2	3
4	5	6	7	8	9	10
11	12	13	14	15	16	17
18	19	20	21	22	23	24
25	26	27	28	29	30	31

Let us thank God for putting us in our one big home of the earth;
let us live happily and harmoniously and do His will,
that our home may become what He wants it to be.

—Paramahansa Yogananda

Mt. Baker, Snoqualmie National Forest, Washington   Photograph by Mary Liz Austin

Meditation is the spring from which God's peace flows into your soul.

—Paramahansa Yogananda

South Falls and maple trees, Silver Creek Canyon, Oregon   Photograph by Terry Donnelly

November/December

28
monday

29
tuesday

New Moon ●

30
wednesday

1
thursday

2
friday

NOVEMBER

S	M	T	W	T	F	S
		1	2	3	4	5
6	7	8	9	10	11	12
13	14	15	16	17	18	19
20	21	22	23	24	25	26
27	28	29	30			

DECEMBER

S	M	T	W	T	F	S
				1	2	3
4	5	6	7	8	9	10
11	12	13	14	15	16	17
18	19	20	21	22	23	24
25	26	27	28	29	30	31

3
saturday

4
sunday

December

5
monday

6
tuesday

7
wednesday

First Quarter ◐

8
thursday

9
friday

10
saturday

11
sunday

DECEMBER

S	M	T	W	T	F	S
				1	2	3
4	5	6	7	8	9	10
11	12	13	14	15	16	17
18	19	20	21	22	23	24
25	26	27	28	29	30	31

JANUARY 2017

S	M	T	W	T	F	S
1	2	3	4	5	6	7
8	9	10	11	12	13	14
15	16	17	18	19	20	21
22	23	24	25	26	27	28
29	30	31				

Like an ocean, the power of God sweeps in, surging through the heart in a cleansing flood, removing all obstructions of delusive doubt, nervousness, and fear.... Then you know that the body is a little bubble of energy in His cosmic sea.

—Paramahansa Yogananda

Sunset light on Cape Kiwanda, Oregon Photograph by Dennis Frates

Teach me to behold Thy face in the mirror of my stillness within.

—Paramahansa Yogananda

Merced River, Yosemite National Park, California   Photograph by Mary Liz Austin

December

12
monday

Full Moon ◯

13
tuesday

14
wednesday

15
thursday

16
friday

DECEMBER

S	M	T	W	T	F	S
				1	2	3
4	5	6	7	8	9	10
11	12	13	14	15	16	17
18	19	20	21	22	23	24
25	26	27	28	29	30	31

17
saturday

JANUARY 2017

S	M	T	W	T	F	S
1	2	3	4	5	6	7
8	9	10	11	12	13	14
15	16	17	18	19	20	21
22	23	24	25	26	27	28
29	30	31				

18
sunday

December

19
monday

20
tuesday
Last Quarter ◑

21
wednesday
Winter Solstice

22
thursday

23
friday

24
saturday
Hanukkah

25
sunday
Christmas

DECEMBER

S	M	T	W	T	F	S
				1	2	3
4	5	6	7	8	9	10
11	12	13	14	15	16	17
18	19	20	21	22	23	24
25	26	27	28	29	30	31

JANUARY 2017

S	M	T	W	T	F	S
1	2	3	4	5	6	7
8	9	10	11	12	13	14
15	16	17	18	19	20	21
22	23	24	25	26	27	28
29	30	31				

Any time your consciousness is attuned to divine realization,
Christ will take birth anew in the cradle of your awakened soul perceptions.
Coming out of the secret fastnesses of Nature, the Omnipresent Christ
reveals to you the wonders of infinite love and wisdom.

—Paramahansa Yogananda

Milky Way over Gates of the Arctic National Park, Alaska Photograph by Arctic-Images/Superstock

Let us forget the sorrows of the past and make up our minds
not to dwell on them in the New Year.
With determination and unflinching will, let us renew our lives,
our good habits, and our successes.

—Paramahansa Yogananda

Arctic fox on west coast of Hudson Bay, Canada Photograph by Roberta Olenick/Grandmaison Photography

December/January

26
monday

Boxing Day (Canada, U.K., Australia, N.Z.)

27
tuesday

28
wednesday

New Moon ●

29
thursday

30
friday

31
saturday

1
sunday

New Year's Day

December

S	M	T	W	T	F	S
				1	2	3
4	5	6	7	8	9	10
11	12	13	14	15	16	17
18	19	20	21	22	23	24
25	26	27	28	29	30	31

January 2017

S	M	T	W	T	F	S
1	2	3	4	5	6	7
8	9	10	11	12	13	14
15	16	17	18	19	20	21
22	23	24	25	26	27	28
29	30	31				

NOTES

ACKNOWLEDGMENTS

We wish to express our sincere appreciation to the following photographers and agencies who contributed to this year's *Inner Reflections* engagement calendar. Following a contributor's name, in parentheses, is the month and a day of the week, or other description, where each photo appears.

AKM Images (3/7, 9/26)

AnimalsAnimals (Cover, 4/11)

Ellen Anon (2/1)

Ken Archer (10/31)

Arctic-Images/SuperStock (12/19)

Mary Liz Austin (2/15, 11/21, 12/12)

Tom Bean/DRK Photo (9/19)

Cliff Beittel (7/18)

Jon Cornforth (8/1)

Terry Donnelly (7/4, 11/28)

DRK Photo (6/13, 9/19)

Guy Edwardes (3/28, 6/20, 7/11)

Tim Fitzharris (11/14)

Dennis Flaherty (1/18, 5/9)

Dennis Frates (2/29, 8/8, 8/22, 12/5)

Daisy Gilardini/Getty Images (5/2)

Grandmaison Photography (6/27, 12/26)

Carl Hanninen /Grandmaison Photography (6/27)

Martin Harvey/DRK Photo (6/13)

John Hendrickson (1/4, 8/29)

William Houghton/AKM Images (9/26)

Cathy and Gordon Illg (9/12)

Jaynes Gallery (1/25)

Adam Jones/Dennis Flaherty Photography (1/18)

Michael Jones/AKM Images (3/7)

Dennis Kirkland/Jaynes Gallery (1/25)

Jackie Klieger (6/6)

Franz Lanting (2/22, 4/4, 5/30)

G. Brad Lewis (2/8)

Robert Lubeck/AnimalsAnimals (4/11)

Kevin McNeal (12/28/15, 1/11, 5/23, 11/7)

Minden Pictures/SuperStock (5/16)

Roberta Olenick/Grandmaison Photography (12/26)

Don Paulson (3/21, 4/18, 10/3)

Photoshot (2/22)

Prisma/SuperStock (9/5)

James Randklev (10/24)

Seth Resnick/SuperStock (10/17)

Fi Rust (3/14)

Steffen & Alexandra Sailer/AnimalsAnimals (Cover)

Anup Shah (7/25, 8/15, 10/10)

SuperStock (5/16, 9/5, 10/17, 12/19)

Michael Wheatley (4/25)

About Paramahansa Yogananda

Paramahansa Yogananda
1893-1952

All the quotes featured in *Inner Reflections* have been selected from the writings of Paramahansa Yogananda, one of the pre-eminent spiritual teachers of the 20th century. Yogananda came to the United States in 1920 as India's delegate to an international congress of religious leaders convening in Boston. He remained in the West for the better part of the next thirty-two years, conducting classes in cities across America, counseling, and creating a monumental body of written work.

Paramahansa Yogananda's life story, *Autobiography of a Yogi*, is considered a modern spiritual classic. It was selected one of "The Top 100 Spiritual Books of the Twentieth Century" in a survey conducted by HarperCollins. A perennial best seller since it was first published in 1946, *Autobiography of a Yogi* has been translated into more than thirty languages and is widely used in college and university courses.

For more information about SRF publications and the teachings of Paramahansa Yogananda, please visit our website:

www.yogananda-srf.org

Self-Realization Fellowship
FOUNDED 1920 BY PARAMAHANSA YOGANANDA

SELF-REALIZATION FELLOWSHIP, the international nonprofit society founded by Paramahansa Yogananda, is dedicated to carrying on his spiritual and humanitarian work — fostering a spirit of greater harmony and understanding among those of all nations and faiths, and introducing truth-seekers around the world to his universal teachings on the ancient science of Yoga.

A SELECTION OF BOOKS BY PARAMAHANSA YOGANANDA

Available at bookstores or from our website:
www.srfbooks.org

Autobiography of a Yogi
(eBook editions also available from Amazon Kindle and Apple iTunes)

Autobiography of a Yogi *(Audiobook, read by Sir Ben Kingsley)*

The Science of Religion

The Law of Success

How You Can Talk With God

Metaphysical Meditations

Where There Is Light: *Insight and Inspiration for Meeting Life's Challenges*

The Yoga of Jesus: *Understanding the Hidden Teachings of the Gospels*

The Yoga of the Bhagavad Gita: *An Introduction to India's Universal Science of God-Realization*

THE COLLECTED TALKS AND ESSAYS

Volume I: Man's Eternal Quest

Volume II: The Divine Romance

Volume III: Journey to Self-realization

SELF-REALIZATION FELLOWSHIP LESSONS

The scientific techniques of meditation taught by Paramahansa Yogananda, including *Kriya Yoga* — as well as his guidance on all aspects of balanced spiritual living — are taught in the *Self-Realization Fellowship Lessons*. For further information, we welcome you to request the free booklet *Undreamed-of Possibilities*.

SELF-REALIZATION FELLOWSHIP

3880 San Rafael Avenue • Los Angeles, CA 90065-3219

TEL (323) 225-2471 • FAX (323) 225-5088

www.yogananda-srf.org

2015

January

s	m	t	w	t	f	s
				1	2	3
4	5	6	7	8	9	10
11	12	13	14	15	16	17
18	19	20	21	22	23	24
25	26	27	28	29	30	31

February

s	m	t	w	t	f	s
1	2	3	4	5	6	7
8	9	10	11	12	13	14
15	16	17	18	19	20	21
22	23	24	25	26	27	28

March

s	m	t	w	t	f	s
1	2	3	4	5	6	7
8	9	10	11	12	13	14
15	16	17	18	19	20	21
22	23	24	25	26	27	28
29	30	31				

April

s	m	t	w	t	f	s
			1	2	3	4
5	6	7	8	9	10	11
12	13	14	15	16	17	18
19	20	21	22	23	24	25
26	27	28	29	30		

May

s	m	t	w	t	f	s
					1	2
3	4	5	6	7	8	9
10	11	12	13	14	15	16
17	18	19	20	21	22	23
24/31	25	26	27	28	29	30

June

s	m	t	w	t	f	s
	1	2	3	4	5	6
7	8	9	10	11	12	13
14	15	16	17	18	19	20
21	22	23	24	25	26	27
28	29	30				

July

s	m	t	w	t	f	s
			1	2	3	4
5	6	7	8	9	10	11
12	13	14	15	16	17	18
19	20	21	22	23	24	25
26	27	28	29	30	31	

August

s	m	t	w	t	f	s
						1
2	3	4	5	6	7	8
9	10	11	12	13	14	15
16	17	18	19	20	21	22
23/30	24/31	25	26	27	28	29

September

s	m	t	w	t	f	s
		1	2	3	4	5
6	7	8	9	10	11	12
13	14	15	16	17	18	19
20	21	22	23	24	25	26
27	28	29	30			

October

s	m	t	w	t	f	s
				1	2	3
4	5	6	7	8	9	10
11	12	13	14	15	16	17
18	19	20	21	22	23	24
25	26	27	28	29	30	31

November

s	m	t	w	t	f	s
1	2	3	4	5	6	7
8	9	10	11	12	13	14
15	16	17	18	19	20	21
22	23	24	25	26	27	28
29	30					

December

s	m	t	w	t	f	s
		1	2	3	4	5
6	7	8	9	10	11	12
13	14	15	16	17	18	19
20	21	22	23	24	25	26
27	28	29	30	31		

2017

January

s	m	t	w	t	f	s
1	2	3	4	5	6	7
8	9	10	11	12	13	14
15	16	17	18	19	20	21
22	23	24	25	26	27	28
29	30	31				

February

s	m	t	w	t	f	s
			1	2	3	4
5	6	7	8	9	10	11
12	13	14	15	16	17	18
19	20	21	22	23	24	25
26	27	28				

March

s	m	t	w	t	f	s
			1	2	3	4
5	6	7	8	9	10	11
12	13	14	15	16	17	18
19	20	21	22	23	24	25
26	27	28	29	30	31	

April

s	m	t	w	t	f	s
						1
2	3	4	5	6	7	8
9	10	11	12	13	14	15
16	17	18	19	20	21	22
23/30	24	25	26	27	28	29

May

s	m	t	w	t	f	s
	1	2	3	4	5	6
7	8	9	10	11	12	13
14	15	16	17	18	19	20
21	22	23	24	25	26	27
28	29	30	31			

June

s	m	t	w	t	f	s
				1	2	3
4	5	6	7	8	9	10
11	12	13	14	15	16	17
18	19	20	21	22	23	24
25	26	27	28	29	30	

July

s	m	t	w	t	f	s
						1
2	3	4	5	6	7	8
9	10	11	12	13	14	15
16	17	18	19	20	21	22
23/30	24/31	25	26	27	28	29

August

s	m	t	w	t	f	s
		1	2	3	4	5
6	7	8	9	10	11	12
13	14	15	16	17	18	19
20	21	22	23	24	25	26
27	28	29	30	31		

September

s	m	t	w	t	f	s
					1	2
3	4	5	6	7	8	9
10	11	12	13	14	15	16
17	18	19	20	21	22	23
24	25	26	27	28	29	30

October

s	m	t	w	t	f	s
1	2	3	4	5	6	7
8	9	10	11	12	13	14
15	16	17	18	19	20	21
22	23	24	25	26	27	28
29	30	31				

November

s	m	t	w	t	f	s
			1	2	3	4
5	6	7	8	9	10	11
12	13	14	15	16	17	18
19	20	21	22	23	24	25
26	27	28	29	30		

December

s	m	t	w	t	f	s
					1	2
3	4	5	6	7	8	9
10	11	12	13	14	15	16
17	18	19	20	21	22	23
24/31	25	26	27	28	29	30

2016

January

s	m	t	w	t	f	s
					1	2
3	4	5	6	7	8	9
10	11	12	13	14	15	16
17	18	19	20	21	22	23
24/31	25	26	27	28	29	30

February

s	m	t	w	t	f	s
	1	2	3	4	5	6
7	8	9	10	11	12	13
14	15	16	17	18	19	20
21	22	23	24	25	26	27
28	29					

March

s	m	t	w	t	f	s
		1	2	3	4	5
6	7	8	9	10	11	12
13	14	15	16	17	18	19
20	21	22	23	24	25	26
27	28	29	30	31		

April

s	m	t	w	t	f	s
					1	2
3	4	5	6	7	8	9
10	11	12	13	14	15	16
17	18	19	20	21	22	23
24	25	26	27	28	29	30

May

s	m	t	w	t	f	s
1	2	3	4	5	6	7
8	9	10	11	12	13	14
15	16	17	18	19	20	21
22	23	24	25	26	27	28
29	30	31				

June

s	m	t	w	t	f	s
			1	2	3	4
5	6	7	8	9	10	11
12	13	14	15	16	17	18
19	20	21	22	23	24	25
26	27	28	29	30		

July

s	m	t	w	t	f	s
					1	2
3	4	5	6	7	8	9
10	11	12	13	14	15	16
17	18	19	20	21	22	23
24/31	25	26	27	28	29	30

August

s	m	t	w	t	f	s
	1	2	3	4	5	6
7	8	9	10	11	12	13
14	15	16	17	18	19	20
21	22	23	24	25	26	27
28	29	30	31			

September

s	m	t	w	t	f	s
				1	2	3
4	5	6	7	8	9	10
11	12	13	14	15	16	17
18	19	20	21	22	23	24
25	26	27	28	29	30	

October

s	m	t	w	t	f	s
						1
2	3	4	5	6	7	8
9	10	11	12	13	14	15
16	17	18	19	20	21	22
23/30	24/31	25	26	27	28	29

November

s	m	t	w	t	f	s
		1	2	3	4	5
6	7	8	9	10	11	12
13	14	15	16	17	18	19
20	21	22	23	24	25	26
27	28	29	30			

December

s	m	t	w	t	f	s
				1	2	3
4	5	6	7	8	9	10
11	12	13	14	15	16	17
18	19	20	21	22	23	24
25	26	27	28	29	30	31

January

Sunday	Monday	Tuesday	Wednesday	Thursday	Friday	Saturday
					1	2
3	4	5	6	7	8	9
10	11	12	13	14	15	16
17	18	19	20	21	22	23
24	25	26	27	28	29	30
31						

Jan. 1 New Year's Day

Jan. 4 Day After New Year's Day (N.Z. – Observed)

Jan. 5 Paramahansa Yogananda's Birthday

Jan. 18 Martin Luther King, Jr.'s Birthday (Observed)

Jan. 26 Australia Day (Australia)

FEBRUARY

Sunday	Monday	Tuesday	Wednesday	Thursday	Friday	Saturday
	1	2	3	4	5	6
7	8	9	10	11	12	13
14	15	16	17	18	19	20
21	22	23	24	25	26	27
28	29					

Feb. 8 Waitangi Day (N.Z. – Observed)
Feb. 12 Lincoln's Birthday
Feb. 14 St. Valentine's Day
Feb. 15 Presidents' Day
Feb. 22 Washington's Birthday

March

Sunday	Monday	Tuesday	Wednesday	Thursday	Friday	Saturday
		1	2	3	4	5
6	7	8	9	10	11	12
13	14	15	16	17	18	19
20	21	22	23	24	25	26
27	28	29	30	31		

March 6 Mothering Sunday (U.K.)
March 7 Paramahansa Yogananda's Mahasamadhi
March 9 Sri Yukteswar's Mahasamadhi
March 13 Daylight Saving Time begins (U.S. and Canada)
March 17 St. Patrick's Day
March 19 Vernal Equinox
March 25 Good Friday
March 27 Daylight Savings Time begins (European Union)
Easter Sunday
March 28 Easter Monday (Canada, U.K., Australia, N.Z.)

April

Sunday	Monday	Tuesday	Wednesday	Thursday	Friday	Saturday
					1	2
3	4	5	6	7	8	9
10	11	12	13	14	15	16
17	18	19	20	21	22	23
24	25	26	27	28	29	30

April 22 Passover begins
Earth Day
April 25 ANZAC Day (Australia and N.Z.)

May

Sunday	Monday	Tuesday	Wednesday	Thursday	Friday	Saturday
1	2	3	4	5	6	7
8	9	10	11	12	13	14
15	16	17	18	19	20	21
22	23	24	25	26	27	28
29	30	31				

May 2 Early May Bank Holiday (U.K.)
May 5 National Day of Prayer
May 8 Mother's Day (U.S., Canada, Australia, N.Z.)
May 10 Sri Yukteswar's Birthday
May 23 Victoria Day (Canada)
May 30 Memorial Day
Spring Bank Holiday (U.K.)

June

Sunday	Monday	Tuesday	Wednesday	Thursday	Friday	Saturday
			1	2	3	4
5	6	7	8	9	10	11
12	13	14	15	16	17	18
19	20	21	22	23	24	25
26	27	28	29	30		

June 6 Queen's Birthday (N.Z.)
June 13 Queen's Birthday (Australia)
June 19 Father's Day (U.S., Canada, U.K.)
June 20 Summer Solstice
June 21 International Day of Yoga

July

Sunday	Monday	Tuesday	Wednesday	Thursday	Friday	Saturday
					1	2
3	4	5	6	7	8	9
10	11	12	13	14	15	16
17	18	19	20	21	22	23
24	25	26	27	28	29	30
31						

July 1 Canada Day (Canada)
July 4 Independence Day
July 25 Mahavatar Babaji Commemoration Day

August

Sunday	Monday	Tuesday	Wednesday	Thursday	Friday	Saturday
	1	2	3	4	5	6
7	8	9	10	11	12	13
14	15	16	17	18	19	20
21	22	23	24	25	26	27
28	29	30	31			

Aug. 1 Summer Bank Holiday (Scotland)
Aug. 25 Janmashtami
Aug. 29 Summer Bank Holiday (England, Wales & N. Ireland)

SEPTEMBER

Sunday	Monday	Tuesday	Wednesday	Thursday	Friday	Saturday
				1	2	3
4	5	6	7	8	9	10
11	12	13	14	15	16	17
18	19	20	21	22	23	24
25	26	27	28	29	30	

Sept. 4 Father's Day (Australia and N.Z.)
Sept. 5 Labor Day (U.S. and Canada)
Sept. 21 U.N. International Day of Peace
Sept. 22 Autumnal Equinox
Sept. 26 Lahiri Mahasaya's Mahasamadhi
Sept. 30 Lahiri Mahasaya's Birthday

October

Sunday	Monday	Tuesday	Wednesday	Thursday	Friday	Saturday
						1
2	3	4	5	6	7	8
9	10	11	12	13	14	15
16	17	18	19	20	21	22
23	24	25	26	27	28	29
30	31					

Oct. 2 Rosh Hashanah
Oct. 10 Columbus Day
Thanksgiving Day (Canada)
Oct. 11 Yom Kippur
Oct. 24 Labour Day (N.Z.)
Oct. 30 Daylight Saving Time ends (European Union)
Oct. 31 Halloween (U.S., Canada, U.K.)

NOVEMBER

Sunday	Monday	Tuesday	Wednesday	Thursday	Friday	Saturday
		1	2	3	4	5
6	7	8	9	10	11	12
13	14	15	16	17	18	19
20	21	22	23	24	25	26
27	28	29	30			

Nov. 6 Daylight Saving Time ends (U.S. and Canada)
Nov. 5 Guy Fawkes Day (England)
Nov. 8 General Election Day
Nov. 11 Veterans Day
Remembrance Day (Canada)
Nov. 13 Remembrance Sunday (U.K.)
Nov. 24 Thanksgiving Day

December

Sunday	Monday	Tuesday	Wednesday	Thursday	Friday	Saturday
				1	2	3
4	5	6	7	8	9	10
11	12	13	14	15	16	17
18	19	20	21	22	23	24
25	26	27	28	29	30	31

Dec. 21 Winter Solstice
Dec. 24 Hanukkah
Dec. 25 Christmas
Dec. 26 Boxing Day (Canada, U.K., Australia, N.Z.)

NOTES

INNER REFLECTIONS

Engagement Calendar 2016

SELECTIONS FROM THE WRITINGS OF

PARAMAHANSA YOGANANDA

SELF-REALIZATION FELLOWSHIP

FRONT COVER:
Whahariki Beach, Golden Bay, New Zealand
Photograph by Steffen & Alexandra Sailer/AnimalsAnimals
Design by Shawn Freeman

NOTE: *Holidays and other observed dates are included for the United States (U.S.), Canada, United Kingdom (U.K.), Australia, and New Zealand (N.Z.).*
Moon phases, equinoxes, and solstices are based on Pacific Standard Time (UTC – 8 hours).

Printed in Italy
4830-J3372